CONTENTS

No Milk! 4

A Different Problem 8

The Reaction 10

Stay Away! 16

Read the Label 18

Grow Up? 20

Words to Know 22

For More Information 23

Index 24

Boldface words appear in Words to Know.

NO MILK!

Do you love cookies and milk? How about cereal with milk? Milk is a common part of many kids' **diets**. But, not everyone can drink milk or eat anything with milk in it! They have a milk allergy.

An allergy is when eating, touching, or breathing in something that's harmless to most people makes you sick.

An allergic **reaction** to milk likely happens because a person's body made antibodies to fight milk **proteins**. Antibodies are special parts of the blood. They fight germs and other matter the body thinks is an **intruder**.

Milk is used to make cheese, ice cream, and yogurt, among other products.

A DIFFERENT PROBLEM

People who are lactose intolerant feel sick when they take in milk. But, they aren't allergic to milk. Their bodies can't break down a sugar called lactose found in milk.

Lactose-free milk is a way for those who are lactose intolerant to still enjoy milk.

THE REACTION

An allergic reaction to milk can occur right away. It can also happen a few hours later. Common allergic reactions to milk include hives and **swelling** around the mouth and eyes.

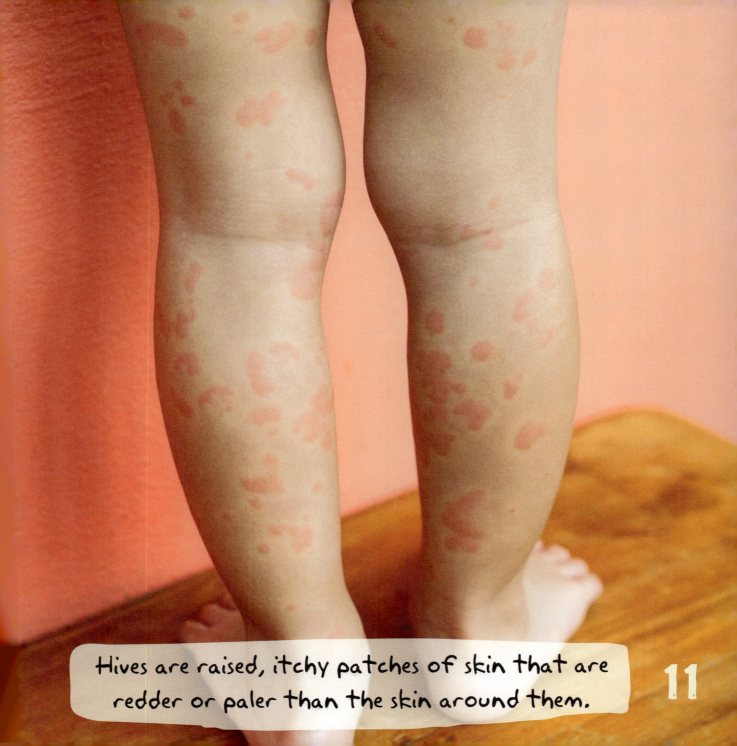

Hives are raised, itchy patches of skin that are redder or paler than the skin around them.

11

If you have a milk allergy, milk products can give you a tummy ache or make you throw up. Some people have trouble breathing and swallowing. If their throat closes up, they might pass out.

Milk from cows is the most common milk allergy. People can also be allergic to goat, buffalo, and sheep's milk!

A doctor is needed if someone has a bad allergic reaction like those listed on page 12. A shot of a drug called epinephrine (eh-puh-NEH-fruhn) can help. People with milk allergies sometimes carry their own shot, just in case.

An epinephrine shot may save the life of someone having a bad allergic reaction.

STAY AWAY

The only way to **avoid** an allergic reaction to milk is to stop taking in any milk. That means you can't drink milk! You also can't eat butter, ice cream, yogurt, or cheese.

Those with a milk allergy might be able to drink almond, oat, or soy milk instead.

READ THE LABEL

Reading food labels is important when you have any food allergy. Those with a milk allergy have to read food labels to make sure a food isn't made with milk. The label may say milk, or another word, such as casein.

Sodium	45mg		
Recommended Daily Allowances (United States)			
Vitamin A	0%	Vitamin C	0%
Calcium	15%	Iron	2%

Nutritional Information

Ingredients: Sugar, non-dairy creamer (corn syrup solids, coconut oil, sodium caseinate (a milk derivative), dipotassium phosphate, maltodextrin, mono- and diglycerides, tricalcium phosphate, silicon dioxide, carrageenan, soy lecithin, salt), whey protein, Arabica coffee, natural and artificial flavoring, tricalcium phosphate, salt.

Allergen Information: Contains milk and soy.

Casein is a milk protein that's in a lot of products—even gum!

GROW UP?

Many kids who have a milk allergy outgrow it by age 8. Most have outgrown the allergy by the time they're a teenager. You may not be able to have a cheese sandwich now, but maybe someday you will!

Milk allergies are one of the most common in children.

21

WORDS TO KNOW

avoid: Stay away from.

diet: The food that a person commonly eats.

intruder: Someone who forces their way into a place they're not wanted.

protein: One of the building blocks of food.

reaction: The way someone responds to something.

swelling: Getting bigger in an uncommon way.

FOR MORE INFORMATION

BOOKS

Orlando, Amanda. *The Easy Allergy-free Cookbook: 85 Recipes Without Gluten, Dairy, Tree Nuts, Peanuts, Eggs, Fish, Shellfish, Soy, Or Wheat.* Emeryville, CA: Rockridge Press, 2022.

Vallepur, Shalini. *I'm Allergic to Dairy.* King's Lynn, UK: BookLife Publishing, 2019.

WEBSITES

Learning About Allergies
kidshealth.org/en/kids/allergies.html
Find out more about allergies here.

Milk Allergy
www.kidswithfoodallergies.org/milk-allergy.aspx
Learn more about having a milk allergy and how to manage it.

Publisher's note to educators and parents: Our editors have carefully reviewed these websites to ensure that they are suitable for students. Many websites change frequently, however, and we cannot guarantee that a site's future contents will continue to meet our high standards of quality and educational value. Be advised that students should be closely supervised whenever they access the internet.

Index

alternative milks, 17
antibodies, 6
epinephrine, 14, 15
food label, 18
hives, 10, 11
lactose intolerant, 8, 9

outgrow allergy, 20
protein, 6
trouble breathing, 12
tummy ache, 12
swelling, 10

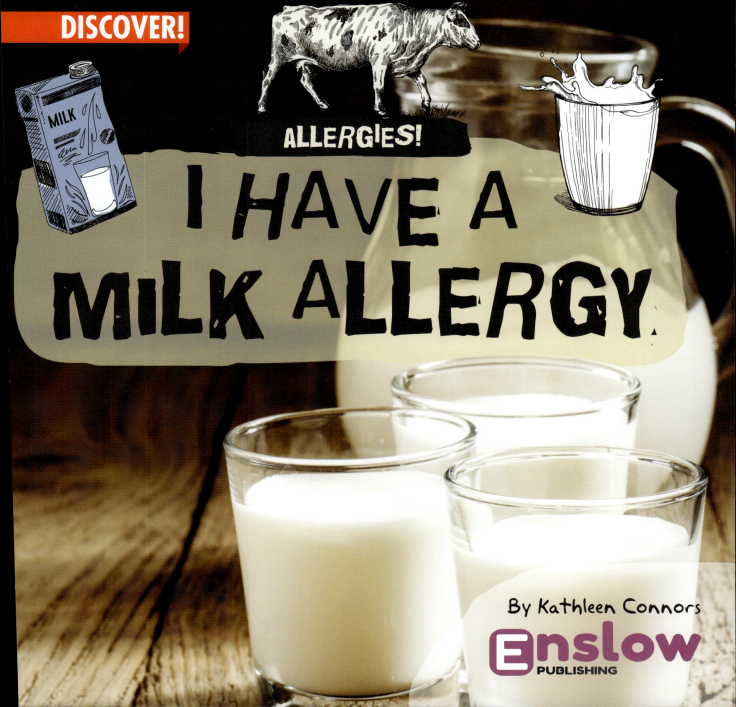

Please visit our website, www.enslow.com. For a free color catalog of all our high-quality books, call toll free 1-800-398-2504 or fax 1-877-980-4454.

Library of Congress Cataloging-in-Publication Data

Names: Connors, Kathleen, author.
Title: I have a milk allergy / Kathleen Connors.
Description: Buffalo, New York : Enslow Publishing, [2024] | Series: Allergies! | Includes bibliographical references and index. | Audience: Grades K-1
Identifiers: LCCN 2022045102 (print) | LCCN 2022045103 (ebook) | ISBN 9781978533783 (library binding) | ISBN 9781978533776 (paperback) | ISBN 9781978533790 (ebook)
Subjects: LCSH: Food allergy in children–Juvenile literature. | Milk–Health aspects–Juvenile literature.
Classification: LCC RJ386.5 .C6635 2024 (print) | LCC RJ386.5 (ebook) | DDC 618.92/975-dc23/eng/20220928
LC record available at https://lccn.loc.gov/2022045102
LC ebook record available at https://lccn.loc.gov/2022045103

Portions of this work were originally authored by Maria Nelson and published as *I'm Allergic to Milk*. All new material this edition authored by Kathleen Connors.

Published in 2024 by
Enslow Publishing
2544 Clinton Street
Buffalo, NY 14224

Copyright © 2024 Enslow Publishing

Designer: Claire Wrazin
Editor: Kristen Nelson

Photo credits: Cover (photo) 5PH/Shutterstock.com; Cover (art, cow) La puma/Shutterstock.com; Cover (art, left), pp. 3, 6, 8, 16, 18, 20 Natalya Levish/Shutterstock.com; Cover (art, right), Series Art (texture) arigato/Shutterstock.com; pp. 4, 10, 12, 22 Mashikomo/Shutterstock.com; p. 5 aleks333/Shutterstock.com; p. 7 margouillat photo/Shutterstock.com; p. 9 Brookgardener/Shutterstock.com; p. 11 Arlee.P/Shutterstock.com; p. 13 polya_olya/Shutterstock.com; p. 15 Andrey_Popov/Shutterstock.com; p. 17 Littlekidmoment/Shutterstock.com; p. 19 STILLFX/Shutterstock.com; p. 21 gpointstudio/Shutterstock.com

All rights reserved. No part of this book may be reproduced in any form without permission in writing from the publisher, except by a reviewer.

Printed in the United States of America

Some of the images in this book illustrate individuals who are models. The depictions do not imply actual situations or events.

CPSIA compliance information: Batch #CS24ENS; For further information contact Enslow Publishing, at 1-800-398-2504.